CONTENTS

ROBOTS

Jonathan Rutland

Published 1979 by Warwick Press, 730 Fifth Avenue,
New York 10019
First published in Great Britain by Ward Lock in 1978
Copyright © 1978 by Grisewood & Dempsey Ltd
Printed in Italy by New Interlitho, Milan
6 5 4 3 2 1 All rights reserved

WARWICK PRESS · NEW YORK

Library of Congress Catalog Card No. 78–67836
ISBN 0–531–09130–9
ISBN 0–531–09115–5 lib. bdg.

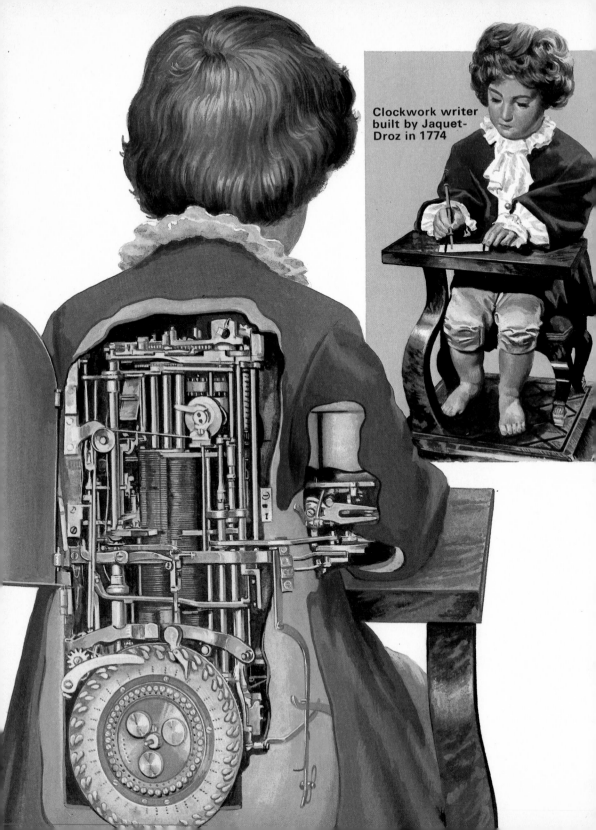

Clockwork writer built by Jaquet-Droz in 1774

Early Robots

A robot is a machine which can "think" for itself. But a human being must build its "brain". And the brain must be "programed" —instructions are built in before the robot can do its work.

Our bodies are wonderful machines. And some robots have parts like those of the human body. They have mechanical arms and legs. They have electronic eyes, ears and brains. But they can only do the jobs they are built for.

The first robot-like machines were clockwork toys. More than 200 years ago a Swiss clockmaker made a life-size doll. It sits at a desk and it can write. Inside the doll is a mass of rods, wires and wheels. These controls move its arm to dip the pen in the ink and write on the paper.

The doll is cleverly made. But it is not a true robot. It is an "automaton". It works by clockwork just like a toy automobile. If an obstacle is in the toy's way, the toy bumps into it. It cannot avoid the obstacle by thinking for itself. If the doll's inkpot is empty, the doll still dips the pen in and goes on writing without ink. It does not "know" the pen is dry.

But the tea maker (below) is very different. If there is no match to light the heater, the kettle does not boil. It does not tip up and the bell does not ring. The tea maker "knows" when its kettle is ready and does not go on working when something goes wrong. It is a true robot.

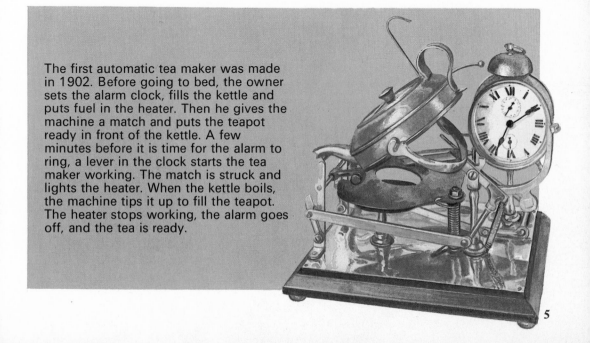

The first automatic tea maker was made in 1902. Before going to bed, the owner sets the alarm clock, fills the kettle and puts fuel in the heater. Then he gives the machine a match and puts the teapot ready in front of the kettle. A few minutes before it is time for the alarm to ring, a lever in the clock starts the tea maker working. The match is struck and lights the heater. When the kettle boils, the machine tips it up to fill the teapot. The heater stops working, the alarm goes off, and the tea is ready.

Robots all Around

There are robots all around us. Some do very complicated jobs like flying airplanes and driving subway trains. And some do one simple job.

When an automatic washing machine is switched on, water pours in. The machine waits until the water is hot before washing the clothes. It does this by "feedback". Information about what is happen-ing is "fed back" into the robot to tell it what to do next.

Our eyes, ears and other senses are our feedback. They tell us what is going on around us. So robots are like people in two ways. They work and they have feedback.

But very few robots look like people. Many are hidden away. Robots control the temperature of our houses, our cookers, our hot water systems. We can set the controls to the temperature we want. The robot does the rest. Its feedback usually

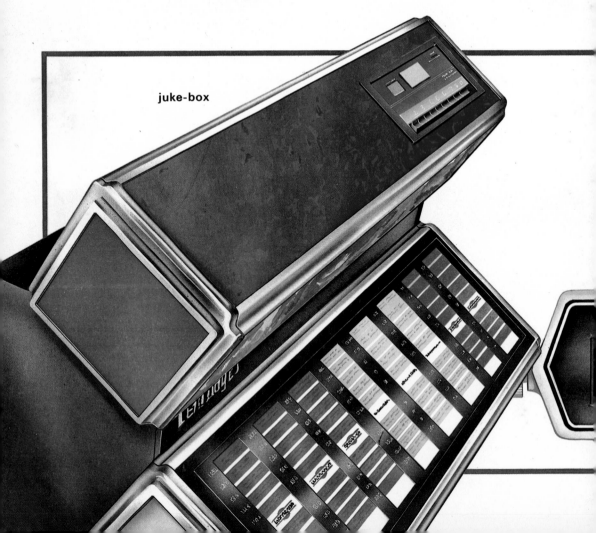

juke-box

comes from a thermostat.

One kind of thermostat is a strip of metal which bends when it gets hot. At the right temperature, it bends just enough to work a switch. This turns off the heat. As the air around it cools, the metal straightens, and this turns the heat on again.

There are robots all around, making our lives easier. Some of them, like the pocket calculator, can work much more quickly than human beings can. And they rarely make mistakes.

traffic lights

automatic washing machine

push-button telephone

digital clock

pocket calculator

Factory Robots

In some ways robots are better than people. They work quickly, but do not make mistakes. They do not get bored doing the same job over and over again. And they never get tired.

So robots are very useful in factories. They can be taught to do many different jobs. First their electronic brains must be shown how the job is done. A person moves the robot's "arms" and "hand" through each part of the job. The robot's brain remembers each move. When the robot is put to work on its own, its brain controls the rods, wheels and motors which move its arm.

When the robot is needed for a new job, its electronic memory is "wiped clean". Then it is taught how to do its new task.

If the robot's hand stops working, or if something gets in the way, it cannot do the next part of the job. So it stops and signals for help. Then a human engineer attends to the fault.

Robots are also used for doing jobs which are dangerous. They can move objects which are too hot or too heavy for people to handle. They can work in places which are too hot or too cold for people. And they are not affected by poisonous fumes or gases.

There are no human workers in this part of an automobile factory. Instead, the work is done by robots. The automobile bodies are moved automatically along the assembly line. One-armed robot welders fix the parts of each body together.

Factory robots can be given different kinds of grippers or "fingers". The robot can move the gripper up and down, and also turn it round.

robot gripper

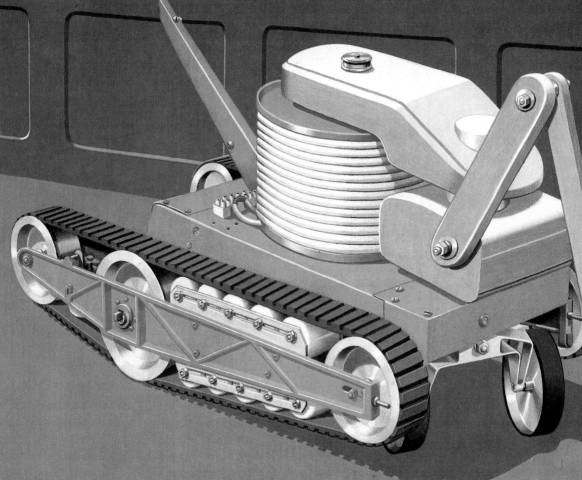

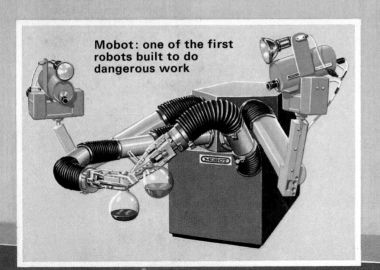

Mobot: one of the first robots built to do dangerous work

Robots in Research

The most "intelligent" robots can move and see. Their eyes are cameras. Their metal fingers can feel shapes and even find out how hot and cold objects are. These robots have computer brains, linked to their eyes and fingers, which control their actions.

These very expensive robots are used in scientific research. They do special jobs, such as handling radio-active materials.

These materials are very dangerous. They give off invisible rays which can harm people. They are far too dangerous to touch, and must be kept in sealed rooms. But they are useful. They are used to make nuclear energy to drive engines and produce electricity. Special robots are needed to handle them.

The Rivet robot can take rods of radioactive metal in and out of special containers. Rivet is a remotely controlled vehicle. Scientists can control Rivet and watch it at work from behind a special glass window.

Another research robot looks just like a person. Its name is Sim. It is a "simulation", an "imitation person". It has a heart, blood, skin, and all the other parts of a human body. But it is made of plastic and metal. Sim is used to teach doctors. They can practise doing operations. Sim can be given an illness, and the doctors can learn how to cure it.

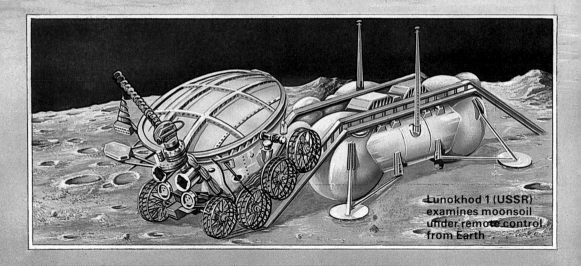

Lunokhod 1 (USSR) examines moonsoil under remote control from Earth

Robot Wanderers

Robots can go to places where human beings would die. They do not need food or air. So they are ideal explorers, traveling in outer space or deep beneath the sea.

Astronauts in a spacecraft rely on the help of robots. Computers, which are robot brains, help control the spacecraft. They help keep it on the right course and make sure that everything works properly. If a piece of equipment goes wrong, they put it right or signal a warning.

Astronauts have visited the Moon, but robot spacecraft have made much longer journeys to other planets. Sometimes the robot spacecraft flies past a planet, taking photographs and making scientific measurements. All this information is then sent back to Earth by radio. More computers help the scientists sort out the many new facts they have learned.

Other robots can land and explore. The Russian Lunokhod was a robot which crawled about the Moon's surface. The American Viking probes landed on Mars. They scooped up soil with long mechanical arms, and tested the soil to see if any plants or animals lived in it.

Robot wanderers explore underwater too. Some have their own computer brains. They "see" by television and can carry out repair work on underwater oil wells.

Other deep-sea robots are controlled by human divers. The underwater bulldozer is being driven by the frogman. It can also be controlled from the ship above. It has bright lights and television cameras at front and back.

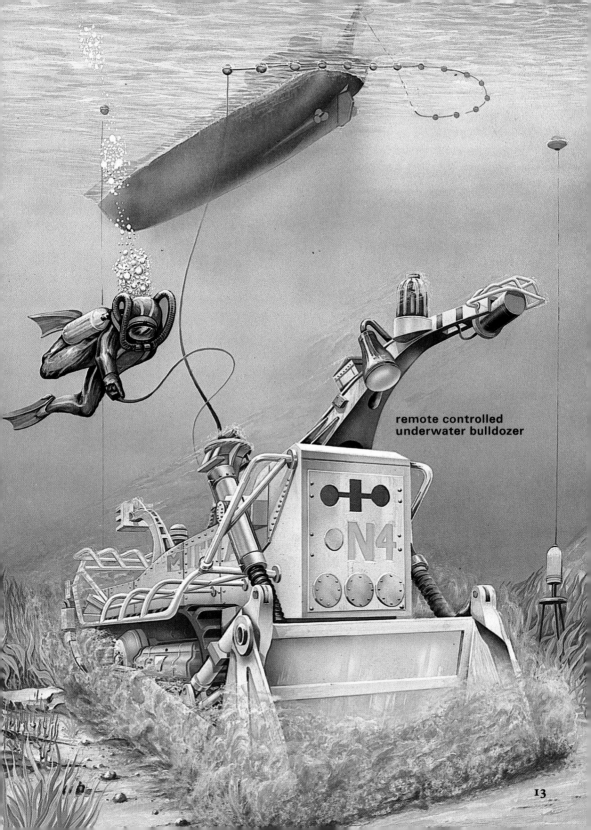

remote controlled
underwater bulldozer

13

An anti-submarine missile drops a torpedo by parachute

The Tornado, a Multi-Role Combat Aircraft, is packed with robot systems

A sea-launched cruise missile springs from the ocean

Robot Warriors

Long ago, wars were fought at close quarters with swords and bows. Today, wars can be fought by remote control, for the modern army has many robot weapons.

Robot brains help the pilot of a jet fighter to find his way, and aim his rockets and bombs accurately. Electronic "eyes" help

pilotless plane

The Russian Scamp system— a mobile missile that can be fired from a tank

guide the plane over hills and valleys at high speed. They also watch out for enemy planes.

Some planes do not need a human pilot at all. They are flown by robot brains or "automatic pilots".

Modern rocket missiles have robot brains to guide them. They hardly ever miss their target. There are anti-aircraft missiles which sense the heat from an enemy plane's engine. No matter how the plane twists and turns it cannot escape.

There are anti-submarine missiles which home in on the sound of a submarine's engine. And there are cruise missiles which are steered thousands of miles by robot brains to land within 30 feet of their target.

A shoulder-launched anti-aircraft missile

RUSH

Robot Brains

The human brain is made up of millions of nerves. They are like electric wires, passing signals to one another. Where two nerves join, there is a kind of switch. A robot has an electronic brain. Inside a robot brain is a mass of electronic switches. Each tiny switch can store a bit of information.

A robot mouse called Theseus has an electronic brain which enables it to find its way through a maze. The first attempt is by trial and error. If one path is a dead end, the mouse turns back and tries another. Eventually, it gets to the end of the maze. When it is put back at the start again, Theseus can run through the maze again and again without a single mistake. It remembers the way.

Without our memories, we could not play games, tell stories, speak, or learn anything at all. No robot can do as many things as a human

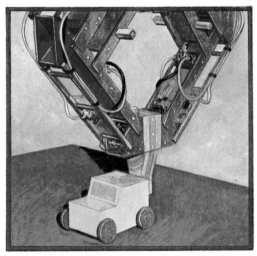

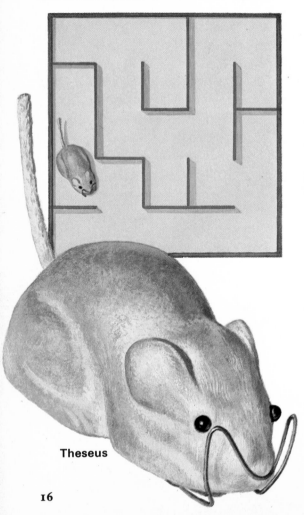

Theseus

Above: This robot, called Freddy, can sort out the pieces of a toy automobile and put them together. You can see his "hand" in the picture. Freddy is rather slow. You could put the toy together more quickly. But future "Freddies" will be able to do such jobs better than we can.

Right: Some computers have been programed to play chess. When a move is made by a human opponent, information is fed to the computer which then decides how to reply. A paper "print-out" shows the positions of the pieces on the chess board.

being can. But robot brains can do some things more quickly than we can.

Today's computers have memories. The information stored inside them is always ready to be used. And they never forget.

A computer can work out in a few seconds a sum which would take a person many hours. So robot brains are very useful for doing all sorts of complicated tasks. They are also used to build even bigger and better robots.

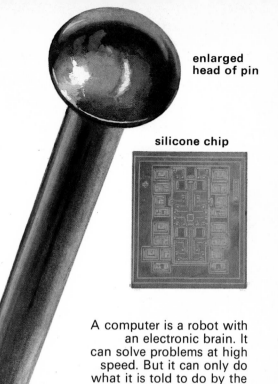

enlarged head of pin

silicone chip

A computer is a robot with an electronic brain. It can solve problems at high speed. But it can only do what it is told to do by the human beings who program and operate it.

The electronic brain in a computer is a store of information and instructions. In some computers all the information is stored in tiny electric circuits printed on silicone chips. Some of these pieces are almost as small as the head of a pin. So a large amount of information can be stored in a very small space.

computer print-out

17

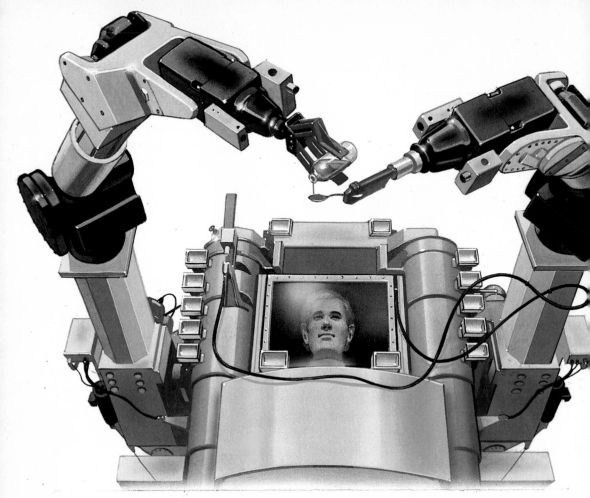

Man plus Machine

Many of the most useful robots are those which can imitate human actions. They can do work that is usually done by people. But some robots do not take the place of people. Instead, they need a person to help them while they work. They need a human brain. So they have an operator inside. But the robot's "muscles" are much stronger than those of the operator.

Inside this robot is a man. The robot protects him from dangerous radioactive metals. He looks out through a thick glass window. When he moves his arms, the robot's arms move too. It can lift heavy weights. But it can also pour medicine into a spoon, without spilling a drop.

The arms of the robot can "grow" so that the operator can reach much farther than usual. And the "fingers" on the arms can be changed to handle different kinds of tools.

The robot also has legs which can extend until it stands more than 26 feet tall. Its job is to work on nuclear engines.

Robot "muscles" and "bones" can make a man stronger. The man in the picture has an extra skeleton made of metal. Its joints are moved by tiny motors. When the man moves, his metal skeleton moves too. With its help he can lift weights very easily because the skeleton gives him extra "muscle" power.

One day we may be able to build robots that move as easily as we do. They might even look like us. "Human" robots are called androids. Androids might have extra strong bodies. Their electronic brains, eyes and ears could even be better than ours. But nobody knows if it will be possible to build robots like these.

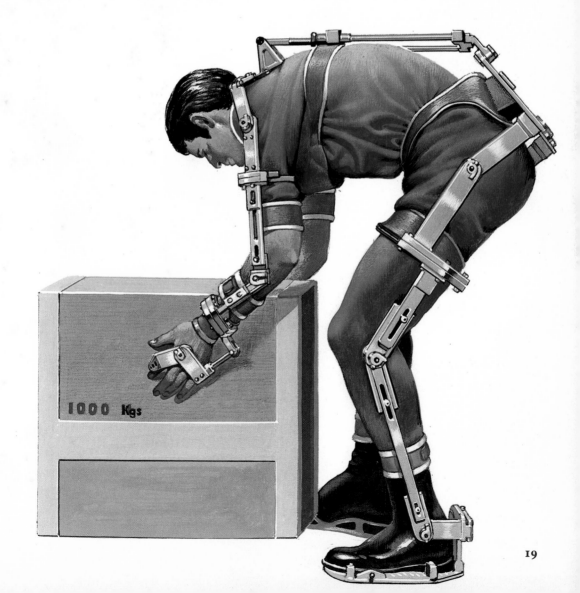

1000 Kgs

Tomorrow's Servants

Today we have many different gadgets in our homes. They make housework and gardening easier. In future we may have robot servants to do all the jobs in the home.

In charge of tomorrow's servants will be a robot brain. It will run the house. It will control other machines electronically. The brain will work vacuum cleaners, lawn mowers, washing machines, food mixers, automatic cookers and other gadgets.

We will be able to give the brain its orders, telling it what jobs to do and when to do them. If we forget to mow the

"Maid Without Tears"

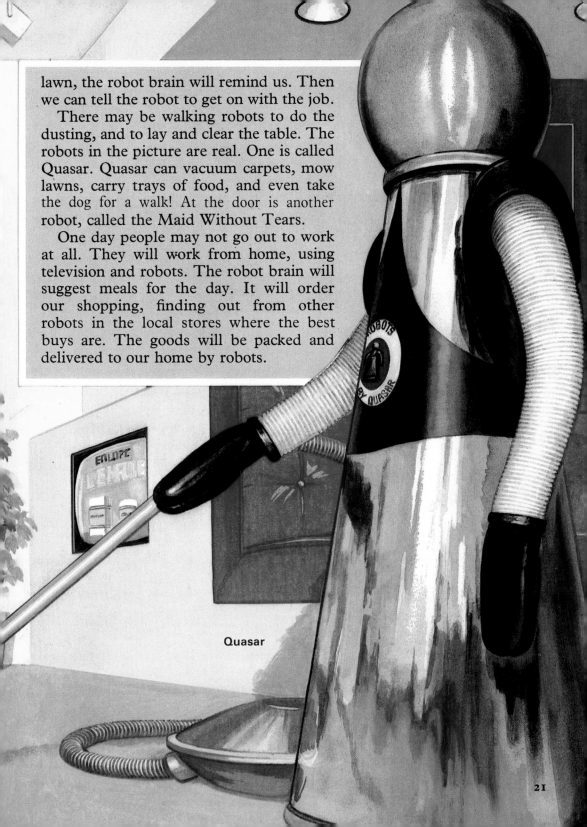

lawn, the robot brain will remind us. Then we can tell the robot to get on with the job.

There may be walking robots to do the dusting, and to lay and clear the table. The robots in the picture are real. One is called Quasar. Quasar can vacuum carpets, mow lawns, carry trays of food, and even take the dog for a walk! At the door is another robot, called the Maid Without Tears.

One day people may not go out to work at all. They will work from home, using television and robots. The robot brain will suggest meals for the day. It will order our shopping, finding out from other robots in the local stores where the best buys are. The goods will be packed and delivered to our home by robots.

Quasar

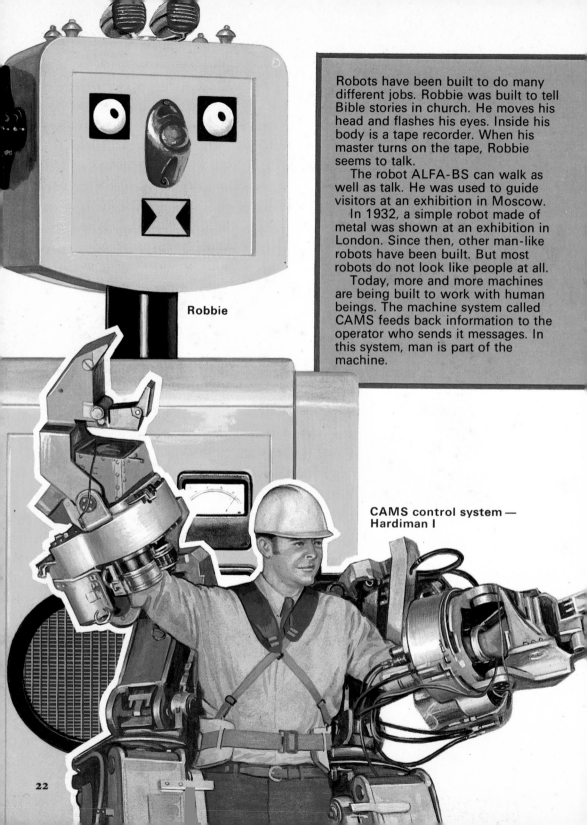

Robbie

Robots have been built to do many different jobs. Robbie was built to tell Bible stories in church. He moves his head and flashes his eyes. Inside his body is a tape recorder. When his master turns on the tape, Robbie seems to talk.

The robot ALFA-BS can walk as well as talk. He was used to guide visitors at an exhibition in Moscow.

In 1932, a simple robot made of metal was shown at an exhibition in London. Since then, other man-like robots have been built. But most robots do not look like people at all.

Today, more and more machines are being built to work with human beings. The machine system called CAMS feeds back information to the operator who sends it messages. In this system, man is part of the machine.

CAMS control system — Hardiman I